Exclusive Distributors:
Music Sales Limited
8/9 Frith Street,
London W1V 5TZ, England.
Music Sales Pty Limited
120 Rothschild Avenue,
Rosebery, NSW 2018,
Australia.

This book © Copyright 1984, 1992 by Wise Publications
Order No.AM37888
ISBN 0-7119-0576-2

MOTOWN CLASSICS

Compiled by Peter Evans
Book design by Pearce Marchbank Studio

Music Sales' complete catalogue lists thousands of titles and is
free from your local music shop, or direct from Music Sales Limited.
Please send a cheque/postal order for £1.50 for postage to:
Music Sales Limited, Newmarket Road, Bury St. Edmunds, Suffolk IP33 3YB.

Printed in the United Kingdom by
J.B. Offset Printers (Marks Tey) Limited, Marks Tey, Essex.

WISE PUBLICATIONS
London/New York/Paris/Sydney

MARVIN GAYE & TAMMI TERRELL
AIN'T NOTHING LIKE THE REAL THING

Words & Music: Nickolas & Valerie Simpson

2.   I read your letters when you're not near
     But they don't move me and they don't groove me
     Like when I hear your sweet voice, whispering in my ear.

DANCING IN THE STREET

MARTHA & THE VANDELLAS

Words & Music: Marvin Gaye, Ivy Hunter & William Stevenson

FOR ONCE IN MY LIFE

Words: Ronald Miller Music: Orlando Murden

2. For Once In My Life I won't let sorrow hurt me,
Not like it's hurt me before,
For once I have something I know won't desert me,
I'm not alone anymore.
For once I can say this is mine, you can't take it,
Long as I know I have love, I can make it,

(Chorus)

I HEARD IT THROUGH THE GRAPEVINE

Words & Music: Norman Whitfield & Barrett Strong

3. People say believe half of what you see
   Oh, and none of what you hear;
   But I can't help but be confused
   If it's true please tell me dear.
   Do you plan to let me go
   For the other guy you loved before?

MY CHERIE AMOUR

Words & Music: Stevie Wonder, Henry Cosby & Sylvia Moy

2. In a cafe or sometimes on a crowded street,
I've been near you but you never noticed me.
My Cherie Amour, won't you tell me how could you ignore,
That behind that little smile I wore,
How I wish that you were mine.

3. Maybe someday you'll see my face among the crowd,
Maybe someday I'll share your little distant cloud.
Oh, Cherie Amour, pretty little one that I adore,
You're the only girl my heart beats for,
How I wish that you were mine.

MY GUY

Words & Music: William 'Smokey' Robinson

TOUCH ME IN THE MORNING

Words: Ron Miller   Music: Michael Masser

THE TRACKS OF MY TEARS

Words & Music: William 'Smokey' Robinson, Marv Tarplin & Warren Moore

oh —— (fade) —————— I need you —————— need —————— you.
                                                              need —————— you.

Hey —————— hey yeah —————————— (Out -

side) I'm mas-que - rad - ing ——————— (In - side) my —— hope —— is

fad - ing; a (Just a clown) oo yeah— a since you put me down, ———— my

smile is my make-up I wear since my break-up with you. Ba - by take a

D.S. al fade

19

YOU ARE THE SUNSHINE OF MY LIFE

Words & Music: Stevie Wonder

Moderately

You are the sun - shine of ___ my life, ___

that's why I'll al - ways be a - round. ___

You are the ap - ple of ___ my eye ___

___ (last time fade) ___

For-ev - er you'll

___ stay in my heart. ___

2. You must have known that I was lonely,
   Because you came to my rescue.
   And I know that this must be heaven;
   How could so much love be inside of you? Whoa.

YOU CAN'T HURRY LOVE

Words & Music: Brian Holland, Lamont Dozier & Eddie Holland

(extra lyrics) You can't hurry love
You just have to wait,
She said love don't come easy
It's a game of give and take.

YOU'RE ALL I NEED TO GET BY

Words & Music: Nickolas Ashford & Valerie Simpson

All, all the joys un-der the sun wrapped up____ in-to one.You're

all, you're all I need _____ you're all I need ____

_____ you're all I need _____ to get by.____

All I need to get by. _____

2. Like an eagle protects his nest, for you I'll do my best.
   Stand by you like a tree, and dare anybody to try and move me.
   Darling in you I found strength where I was torn down.
   Don't know what's in store, but together we can open any door.

3. Just to do what's good for you, and inspire you a little higher.
   I know you can make a man out of a soul that did'nt have a goal
   'Cause we, we got the right foundation, and with love and
   Determination, you're all, you're all I want to strive for;
   And do a little more all, all the joys under the sun,
   Wrapped up into one, you're all, you're all I need,
   You're all I need, You're all I need To get by
   All I need to get by.

NEVER CAN SAY GOODBYE

Words & Music: Clifton Davis

2. Ev'ry time I think I've had enough and start heading for the door,
   There's very strange vibrations, piercing me right to the core. It says
   Turn around you fool you know you love her more and more.

3. I keep thinkin' that our problems soon are all gonna work out,
   But there's that same unhappy feelin', there's that anguish, there's that
   Doubt. It's that same old dizzy hang-up can't do with you or without.

HOW SWEET IT IS (TO BE LOVED BY YOU)

Words & Music: Brian Holland, Lamont Dozier & Eddie Holland

and thank you, ba - by. Hey now ___ how sweet it is ___ to be ___ loved by

you ___ oh, ba - by, _____ how sweet it is ___ to be ___ loved by

you. ___ Yes it is.
(fade)

Ba - by ___ you were bet-ter to me than I've

been to my - self ___ for me ___ there's you and no - bod - y _____ else.

Stop ___ and thank you ba - by I wan-na stop ___ and thank you ba - by. Oh, ___

HIGHER GROUND

Words & Music: Stevie Wonder

2. Powers, keep on lyin', while your people keep on dyin!
   World, keep on turnin' 'cause it won't be too long.

3. Teachers, keep on teachin! Preachers, keep on preachin!
   World, keep on turnin' 'cause it won't be too long.

4. Lovers, keep on lovin! Believers keep on believin!
   Sleepers, just stop sleepin' 'cause it won't be too long.

Don't you let nobody bring you down.
They'll sho' nuff try.
God is gonna show you Higher Ground.
He's the only friend you have around.

WHERE DID OUR LOVE GO?

Words & Music: Brian Holland, Lamont Dozier & Eddie Holland

DIANA ROSS
AIN'T NO MOUNTAIN HIGH ENOUGH

Words & Music: Nickolas & Valerie Simpson

2. I set you free
    I told you you could always count on me
    From that day on, I made a vow,
    I'll be there when you want me,
    Some way, some how.
    'Cause baby there (Chorus)

3. My love is alive
    Way down in my heart
    Although we are miles apart
    If you ever need a helping hand,
    I'll be there on the double
    As fast as I can.
    Don't you know that there (Chorus)

LET'S GET IT ON

Words & Music: Marvin Gaye & Ed Townsend

BABY LOVE

Words & Music: Brian Holland, Lamont Dozier & Eddie Holland

SUPERSTITION

Words & Music: Stevie Wonder

2. Very superstitious, nothing more to say.
Very superstitious, the devil's on his way.
Thirteen month-old baby broke the lookin' glass.
Seven years of bad luck, the good things in your past.
When you believe in things that you don't understand then you suffer.
Superstition ain't the way.

WHAT BECOMES OF THE BROKEN HEARTED?

Words & Music: James Dean, Paul Riser, William Weatherspoon   Arranged: Dave Stewart

I HEAR A SYMPHONY

Words & Music: Brian Holland, Lamont Dozier & Eddie Holland

THREE TIMES A LADY

Words & Music: Lionel Richie

come to the end of our rain - bow,
live my life o - ver a - gain dear,

there's some-thing I must say out loud.
I'd spend each and ev-'ry mo - ment with you.

1. 2. You're once, twice,
3. Instrumental

three times a la - dy. And I love

three times _____ a la-dy ____ I love you, _____ I love ____ you. _____

mf   poco rit.   8va - - - - -

(When) we are together
The moments I cherish.
With ev'ry beat of my heart.
To touch you, to hold you
To feel you, to need you
There's nothing to keep us apart.

WITH YOU I'M BORN AGAIN

Words: Carol Conners   Music: David Shire

A PLACE IN THE SUN

Words: Ronald Miller Music: Bryan Wells

2. Like an old dusty road I get weary from the load
Movin' on, movin' on.
Like this tired troubled earth I've been rollin' since my birth
Movin' on, movin' on.
(Chorus)

14851 1/93

The Beatles

Enya

Phil Collins

Van Morrison

Bob Dylan

Sting

Paul Simon

Tracy Chapman

Eric Clapton

Pink Floyd

New Kids On The Block

Bryan Adams

Tina Turner

Elton John

Bee Gees

Whitney Houston

AC/DC

Bringing you the
words

All the latest in rock and pop.
Plus the brightest and best in West
End show scores. Music books for
every instrument under the sun.
And exciting new teach-yourself
ideas like "Let's Play Keyboard" -
in cassette/book packs, or on video.
Available from all good music shops.

and
music

Music Sales' complete
catalogue lists thousands of
titles and is available free
from your local music shop,
or direct from Music Sales
Limited. Please send a
cheque or postal order for
£1.50 (for postage) to:

Music Sales Limited
Newmarket Road,
Bury St Edmunds,
Suffolk IP33 3YB

Buddy

Five Guys Named Moe

Les Misérables

West Side Story

Phantom Of The Opera

Show Boat

The Rocky Horror Show

**Bringing you the
world's best music.**

Brothers in Arms

E F# B Bsus4?

D#m/A G#m D#m

E F#sus4 F#

Verse: G#m D#m E

"your valleys your farms"

C#m7 "Brothers in

F# sus4 F# G#m E

Arms"

F#sus4 F#

G#m E G#m E G#m E

C#m G#m sus2